FINISHING LINE PRESS

www.finishinglinepress.com

Touch My Head Softly

poems by

Eileen P. Kennedy

Finishing Line Press
Georgetown, Kentucky

Touch My Head Softly

ACKNOWLEDGMENTS

The author gratefully acknowledges the following journals and societies for
publishing, sometimes in a different form, or honoring, the following poems
included in this collection:

"Dream of My Lover," published in *Seven Hills Review* 2018. Second Prize in
Penumbra Haiku Poetry Contest.
"Eulogy for the Costa Rican Ghosts," published in *Banshees* (Flutter Press,
2015). Nominated for the 2015 Pushcart Prize.
"Fleeing," published in *Muse and Stone*, Spring 2009.
"Medicated," published in the *Tribeca Poetry Review,* 2014.
"*Muerte*," published in *Banshees* (Flutter Press, 2015).

Many thanks to the Forbes Library Writing Room, Pioneer Valley
Cohousing Writers, the Florence Poets Society, Robin Barber, Preston M.
Browning, Jr., Ellen Coleman, Carol Edelstein, Cheryl J. Fish, Eugene E.
Tencza, and all the writers in my groups for their support.

Publisher: Leah Huete de Maines
Editor: Christen Kincaid
Cover Art and Design: Jasmine Hernández, bezierbee@gmail.com
Author Photo: Eugene E. Tencza

Order online: www.finishinglinepress.com
also available on amazon.com

Author inquiries and mail orders:
Finishing Line Press
PO Box 1626
Georgetown, Kentucky 40324
USA

Table of Contents

This book is dedicated to the people living with Alzheimer's Disease and their families and caregivers.*

I.   Beginning

The First Decade of the Twenty-First Century

Harry Potter emerged as a cultural icon. I earned a doctorate. Al Gore won the popular vote. George W. Bush became president. I began a full-time faculty position. Al Qaeda terrorists killed nearly 3,000 people. My son navigated high school with a string orchestra and two heartbreaks. Hippies were out. Hipsters were in. Weapons of mass destruction were touted. I dated a math professor. The iPhone rose. Land lines declined. Vladimir Putin was elected President of Russia. You were tenured as an associate professor. Britney Spears turned into a Pop Princess. The Treasury Department bailed out the banks with 700 billion dollars. My son traversed college in Montreal. Daniel Ortega was again elected President of Nicaragua. We looked at houses in Mexico. Soap operas tanked. You were diagnosed with Early Onset Alzheimer's. Torture porn thrived with the *Texas Chainsaw Massacre* and *Saw*. We went to couple's therapy. Greenhouse gas emissions skyrocketed. You underwent unsuccessful alternate therapies. Barack Obama was elected the first black president. My son moved to Ireland. We went to visit. Life ended on *Lost*. You died of Alzheimer's.

Getting Through the Night

What is it about you
that feels like home?

If I say listen to that,
you will have already heard. We are able
to finish each other's sentences. The stories
we tell, true or false,
define who we are. They plait our existence
like a braid,
a blaze of meaning
in every strand.

Feel me with your hands
until words are not needed.
Place the mantle of possibility
around my shoulders. Touch
my head softly
till this long night is over.

Dream of My Lover

You hold me wading
the river rushing below
I cradle your shoes

Facsimile of Passion

My fingers touch the page,
the pen rises,
body poised over desk.

The bamboo forms a barrier
around the heliconia,
protecting it from wind in the night.
Knocking and calling to the squall to stop,
it studies the splendor of the bloom.

So too, this letter is protected,
wrapped in a vessel of intention
closed with waxy seal.

It is opened by you
with ink-smell intimacy.

I see you pensive,
letter in hand.

Later and Before

When I think of Oaxaca
I remember the *Zócalo*
where they sold *pipa del agua*
and chocolate dripping from paper cups.
Where Sunday afternoons brought older couples swaying tall salsa
to the discordant strains of the band.
Where the dark-walled church's stained glass windows
struggled with the odd ray of light.
Where the ghost of D.H. Lawrence
wrote in that park about *Zapotec* mornings.
Where you read him aloud to me there.
Where you sat next to me on the bench.
Where I looked up and you sent a smile.

Later there was so much darkness
even the Mexican sun
couldn't break through.

But that day, that day
you murmur to yourself
of the glory of the words
shimmering on the page.
Sugar birds sing the praises.

Gratitude

We are in Nicoya, the horses passing
through the backdrop of dusk
so strong I want to cut across,
riding the jets of light.
The warmth fervent,
fragrance overtakes me.

Here, early sunset settles
on searing afternoon.
January slides to soft orange,
mourning the heat that goes.

You appear different, flushed.
We bicker over nothing.
I don't know these lips
or perhaps never did.

I drink too much wine
and forget where I buried
my heart on the beach.

These years together are better and worse than those ahead. One of us
will die while the other stays and remembers. Better in that I don't yet
understand the magnitude of loss; worse in that I don't yet know what
we would one day lose. Still we argue, risking everything.

A sad refrain,
the moon rises
to sign my teardrop.

rails and ties

you melt me to hot honey
dripping my essence
till i'm dry and crackling
in the absence of your arms

dripping my essence
a covered tibetan scroll painting
in the absence of your arms
my open lips miss the rich sap

a covered tibetan scroll painting
i feel your breath
my open lips miss the rich sap
limbs opaque

i feel your breath
a wobbling gait running
limbs opaque
yielding my place

a wobbling gait running
i wish you were a pebble i could skim on desolation pond
yielding my place
sinking and disappearing in the cold

i wish you were a pebble i could skim on desolation pond
but you are track to my rails and ties
sinking and disappearing in the cold
i follow you to my wreck

you are track to my ties and rails
i miss your touch
i follow you to my wreck
leaving myself behind

i miss your arms
yielding my place
i follow you to my wreck
you melt me like hot honey

The Empty Whole of Need

Schumann's horn concerto   sound streams
notes move like smoke bush   melody pulsing
melancholic depression   elation   delusion
6/8 time   triple figure pick up
viola strains on top of mountain.
In séance, he communicates with the spirits.
The Ouija spells out his end.
He goes after the premiere to a mental asylum
and dies at 46.

How did his pianist wife feel?
Did she wither and fall like a leaf?
Did she feel the empty whole of need?
Did her grief become pipe smoke and musical notes?
Was his death the bird in the cave that flew her pain away?
Or like tonight, did the ghost of harmonic strains
filter the field and quiet the breeze?

The Bird Feeder

The tabby waits below, tail twitching
for the élan of the woodpecker.
Capturing his prey, throat in mouth,
there is little struggle. The bird's beak drops
as the feline yanks feathers
from its neck. The woodpecker
provides food for mate and offspring. This predator,
fed by its owner, wants only hunt and blood.

I ask you to come, but your breath stops your movement.
Couldn't you be more like the cat and lunge forward,
rather than the bird lying back with stifled gape? Couldn't you
look ahead and feel the pulse as you leap?

Instead you lie back in your chair,
stare blank,
memory rotting like a log in late winter.

Does the angel
whispering in your ear
have a better invitation than mine?

Fleeing

Hearing gaiety,
voices outside,
I poise to escape.
You return too soon,
coffee cups in tow.

II.   Year

Year

December
You wake in the night and fall. You can't remember where the bathroom is.

***

January
We eat dinner at *Rosa Mexicano*. You order *guacamole*. "I found out what it is," you say, "It's Early Onset Alzheimer's."

***

February
We fly to Oaxaca. You ask, in your impeccable Spanish, for a real estate agent. I argue that we should put off our plans to move to Mexico. You throw your airline tickets
across the room.

***

March
In the medical office, the curtains and carpets new, the doctor says, "the disease is progressing faster than we thought, despite the Aricept." A drug that causes you to projectile vomit and shit before you make it to the toilet does not stop the attack on your mind.

***

April
I take your car and drive around with the windows closed.
In the interior darkness, I scream. No one hears me.
I keep screaming.

***

May
We have dinner at your friend's house. Over cheese and crackers, you ask him to help you. We discuss how he will help you. He says he'll help you when you are no longer aware. Your friend, a doctor, will check you into his hospital. He'll help you die comfortably. I leave the table and throw up.

***

June
I wake in the night. You stare blankly at me and ask,
"Who are you?" I say,
"Go back to sleep."

***

July

You accuse me of sleeping with your graduate assistant. I yell, "I did
not cheat on you, I am too busy cleaning up your shit and talking to
your doctors to even think about sex." Your graduate assistant
shadows your Advanced Mathematics, while you teach
to make sure you don't make noticeable errors.

***

August

You wake up happy and say, "Let's go to the Metropolitan.
We'll see the Primitive Art." I remember
who you are.

***

September

We talk out our problems with a therapist. I try to speak calmly about
your accusations. You yell "Liar," repeatedly.
I walk out.

***

October

I call you and you scream, "Don't call again." You slam down the phone.
I call a mutual friend. She says she'll do what she can.
You die in the hospital.

***

November

I attend the memorial service in shock. Your death certificate says
you died in the morning with your friend as attending physician.
I sob thinking of your death.

***

December

I have a dream of you making love to me
the way you used to. I come across some old pictures
and then put them away.

Today

You lie still in your bed
The sleeping pill has made you calm
You know who I am today
So I am content

The sleeping pill has made you calm
You have stopped flailing and shouting
So I am content
To be by your side

Your flailing and shouting has stopped
The accusations too
I am at your side
When you don't know me at all

You accuse me of infidelity
You know who I am today
You don't know me at all
You lie in your bed

Medicated

Tethered to a catheter
my despondent *compadre*
takes so many pills
they could not
possibly know where
to go in his deflated body.
Confused,
the chemicals trek on
like sled dogs in summer
strapped to a luge
nowhere to go
thinking
they would never
come home.

I offer coffee
and *simpático*
and receive back
an incredulous smile.

Vespers

The bells ring, the light
nearly spent, a few hymns remain.
I waste too much time
longing for who you used to be,
who I used to be. We had
summer in us. Now it is
winter. Watching you
wither in front of me, the trees
bare. Strewn branches lie
where swallows once sang.

Snow Village in a Globe

In the shadowed corner,
you mumble, "Where are they?"
propped up on pillows in a white room.

Memory a snow village in a globe
shaken up, floating.

The world comes in recollections
of a red canopy
of an African mother sculpture
of a Oaxacan tapestry
with or without familiarity.

Hospital bed,
crack in ceiling,
perennial tv,
yellow and orange flowers.
No summer, winter, spring, fall.

I wheel you to the solarium,
gurney with saline attached.
Time slows
as I read to you *One Hundred Years of Solitude.*

Looking out to the sea,
an unrelenting grey,
but you see white lilies
surviving frost.

Only Human

The spider spins on my porch
each morning. I take the web down and she
replaces it. Sometimes the same,
sometimes different.

I would spin for you
a house with my body,
a mansion laced in sheltered space
a silver-threaded cocoon.

I would free you
with my desire
casting a balloon net,
floating in the updraft.

I would defeat this disease
that destroys your mind,
your tongue, your dazed body
with the power of my love.

I would write your story better,
by placing the words so carefully. Watch
as the sound of my voice
reaches your eyes and you know who I am.

Dispatch for the Missing

There are many places
that feel you gone
vacant coat pegs
drained Miller bottle
cigarette scent
blank picture frame
wordless paper.

Drying my throat,
my skin parched
I need you like water.
Fill me. Pour me
a waterfall.
Drench places
where I am empty.

III.   Ending

Muerte

Gone sudden and swift
I recall now head askew
eyes expectant fierce

Banishing the Need for Touch

In Mexico, *Día de los Muertos*
welcomes back the dead.
You ride my pain to revisit.

Friends send greetings.
A bouquet of lilies, a sympathy card,
keeps you here.

I place your photo in the card
to remind me
your anger is gone,
not in my bed,
not in my heart.

The Mexicans get rid of the body in a day
banishing the need for touch.
The service for my friend begins,
the rain,
the umbrellas.

A funeral processioner, I follow
behind a hearse,
specter vanishing into rain.

Quatern for the Dead

You died without saying goodbye.
I missed you at the hospital.
We worked it out in therapy.
Then you left by slipping away.

The phone did not ring that morning.
You died without saying goodbye.
You did not discern who I was
the last time. You saw and looked down.

The service had many people.
Your colleagues and students appeared.
You died without saying goodbye.
They said you were an eminent

teacher. I knew the end was near,
by your look and wasted body.
They said you were quiet that day.
You died without saying goodbye.

On Your Cremation

The day you were cremated
the seagulls flew overhead
and landed on the beach at your house.

I wasn't at the cremation
which I heard was small
with little ceremony.

Everyone dies at some point
I know, but I wasn't ready
for your death when it happened.

I went to the Memorial Service
where there were many
of your buddies and students.

They said kind things about you
what a caring teacher
and friend you were.

The seagulls swooped into your garden
and ate the berries you planted
by the fence next to the saltbush.

Memorial

So many poems about tombstones.

In the shadow of Ben Bulben,
Billy Collins leans on Yeats'
swirling the Sligo mist.

In a California cemetery,
Sharon Olds sits on her father's
washing the corner with her tears.

In rural New Hampshire,
Donald Hall returns to Jane's
obsessing like a homing pigeon.

In the silence of the missing,
your urn sits
bone, dirt, marrow, skin in ashes,
without grave
without headstone
without ceremony.

Six Months After

There are things I wanted to tell you. The day of your cremation
the seagulls swooped down and ate the berries you planted by the
saltbush.

> I went to your Memorial Service. Your colleagues
> said you were the most accomplished
> mathematician they knew. Your students called
> you a patient teacher. Your friends talked about
> the fundraiser you made for the Dominican
> plane crash survivors.

At first, in my anger, I wanted to shoot the seagulls, but I didn't have
a gun.

> After you died, I stopped writing poetry. But I
> am starting again, maybe now.

Our years together swept by in a morning, each mourning a year.

> The weeds in your garden keep growing. The bay
> is frozen on the edges, with the ice almost gone.

On warm days, I remember the way we made love in the afternoon,
your hair straggling out of its ponytail. I dreamt you were ninety, and
sleeping beside me, your strong features still recognizable.

> I finally stopped calling your phone.

Some Tithonia bloomed, but lodged on the ground after frost.

> My grief, with its own language, repeats as easy as the
> sea breeze passing through the curtain.

Your snowdrops came up outside the front door. The seagulls
returned to your yard and ate the buds before the berries grew.

Eulogy for the Costa Rican Ghosts

One was young, losing himself under a motorcycle.
Another escaped by her own hand.
Another held on to life through suffocating breath
and piercing jabs in the chest.
Another went unceremoniously in his sleep.

The artist ghosts linger beyond the throbbing beauty.
They land in unforeseen places
by an empty table or bed stand at night
as confused as the living about
where they've gone and what they'll do.

Knocking bamboo ushers in their moans.
Neither missing nor white,
they wonder who you are and what you are doing
and why life has left them and spared you
imperfect as you are.

I feel their aching in the night air
their souls shaking in the tropical trees.
I remember their presence here
and bear them closer as time goes by
my years stealing to inevitable death.

Their tenderness hovers through all the grandeur.
Sanguine flowers evoke their blood.
Vultures fly their memories in the clouded sky.
Arid earth recalls the ash of their decomposed bodies.
Inscribing a silent mantra, I honor who they were.

Cento on Memory

Remorse is memory awake.
Down in the flood of remembrance,
I weep like a child for the past.

I remember, I remember,
the house where I was born
with heart as calm as lakes
that sleep in a frosty moonlight glistening.

I hear the noise of many waters far below,
mixing memory and desire, stirring
dull roots with spring rain.
Through the sad dark, the slowly ebbing tide
breaks on a barren shore.
For who can hold youth,
or perfume, or the moon's gold?

I fling my past behind me like a robe,
dare not indulge in memory's rapturous pain.
To walk the world forever for my sake,
and in each chamber, find me gone.
I hear your words in mournful cadence toll
with ravings wondrous and chaotic
till I might come back again.

The moments pass and pass.
I faint in this obscurity,
the dewy dawn of memory.

Lines in the poem from:
Emily Dickinson; D.H. Lawrence; Thomas Hood; William Wordsworth;
James Joyce; T.S. Eliot; Katherine Mansfield; Sara Teasdale; Ella Wheeler
Wilcox; Emily Brontë; Edna St. Vincent Millay; Amy Lowell; Aleksandr
Pushkin; Aldous Huxley; W.B. Yeats; Alfred, Lord Tennyson.

Year After

January
A galaxy is born this night
You lived on a beach road
I am far from you now in my *casita*
I cry thinking of your death

February
You lived on a beach road
I sit at my desk until dusk
I cry thinking of not being at your death
The sunset a backdrop of sorrow

March
I sit at my desk until twilight
What did you know of death
The sunset sighs green and violet
I remember the blue coverlet

April
What do I know of death
I am far from you now in my home
I remember the canopy bed
Night where a galaxy begins

May
It's cheerless in Massachusetts
I miss the sun in Costa Rica
You told me to let go of things
I breathe rain lightning and sadness

June
The sun is not like Costa Rica
You wanted your mind to stop waning
My sadness is rain and lightning
You told me you didn't love me

July
You wanted your mind to stop failing
You asked your friend to help you
You didn't love me anymore
My heart snapped like a twig

August
You asked your friend to help you
You died without fear
My heart snapped like a twig
It's dismal in Massachusetts

September
Night where a galaxy starts
You couldn't help tearing things apart
All is leafless in the trees before me
In therapy we tried to work things out

October
You couldn't help separating us
You remember your father's beatings
We didn't work things out in therapy
You stay away more and more

November
You recall your father's violence
You die in the hospital
You stayed away all the time
I was not at the death

December
Your friend was there in the hospital
You died unafraid
I went to the service
Night where a galaxy arises

Endgame

When a star dies in the sky
Bribri believe
that a beast spirit is formed. I like

to think of you
as a howler monkey
screeching wild as a new globe starts.

It went badly.
I loved you, what you
were before it took your mind.
Everything blown in the *Papagayo*,
I would follow you again,
trailing your dark star.

Eileen P. Kennedy grew up in New York City, where she also raised her son. She got her undergraduate degree in journalism from the University of Missouri at Columbia and her doctorate in language and literacy from Fordham University. She taught for many years on the faculty of the City University of New York at Medgar Evers College, Eugenio María de Hostos Community College and Kingsborough Community College. She has been writing since she was eight years old.

Eileen's former partner, a college professor, died from Early Onset Alzheimer's Disease at the age of 69. He had a brilliant mind and was beloved by his students. Over a short period, he lost his memory, developed dementia, and died. This collection of poems is an attempt for her to process what happened.

Eileen was nominated for a Pushcart Prize for her first book of poetry, *Banshees* (Flutter Press, 2015.) This book was also awarded Second Prize from the Wordwrite Book Awards in Poetry. She was given Honorable Mention in Formal Poetry from the Tom Howard/ Margaret Reid Poetry Contest in 2016 and from the New England, New York and London Book Festivals. She was a finalist for the Concrete Wolf Louis Award and the *Crosswinds Poetry Journal* 2017 Poetry Contest. Her poetry has appeared in more than 25 literary journals. She has also published a textbook, as well as fiction and nonfiction.

She has been awarded residencies at the Woodstock Byrdcliffe Guild, Woodstock, NY; AIR 'Le Parc,' Pampellonne, France; and the Hambidge Center for Creative Arts and Sciences, Rabun Gap, Georgia. She lives in Amherst, Massachusetts, with the ghost of Emily Dickinson. She spends time canoeing, hiking, and writing. She reads her work widely in community and academic settings and teaches poetry locally. She winters in Costa Rica. More at EileenPKennedy.com.

Also by Eileen P. Kennedy

Banshees (Flutter Press, 2015)

On *Banshees*:

"Like the mythological banshees of the book's title, Eileen P. Kennedy's poems arrive as messengers, for they are passionate, fierce, and insistent about what they've witnessed. And although much of this collection carries an elegiac tone, the poet also hears 'ancient laughter/between the lines.' These contrasts comprise a universe that feels both very old and simultaneously of our present, and reflects timeless truths and experiences such as love and death and longing."

—Holly Wren Spaulding
Author of *Pilgrim* and *The Grass Impossibly*

"Eileen P. Kennedy's poetry is suffused with images of aging and death. In 'Psalm of the Writer,' the writer suggests 'supplications upward from the mausoleum of the throat,' a beautiful image suggesting the pathos of human yearning for connection, for communication, for eternal life amidst separation and loss. In 'Muerte,' three lines that speak bluntly, matter-of-factly of death: 'Gone sudden and swift/I recall now head askew/eyes expectant fierce.'

In 19 brief poems, Kennedy touches on all the big topics: friendship, love, aging, death, religion, politics, and poetry itself. 'I meet you in what I write,' she says in 'Elegy for the Poet.' We meet ourselves in what she writes."

—Preston M. Browning, Jr.
Associate Professor Emeritus of English,
University of Illinois at Chicago
Director, Wellspring House Writers Retreat